Poems Of A Cynical Introvert

Melanie Kennedy

India | USA | UK

The Rambling Poems Of A Cynical Introvert
© 2023 Melanie Kennedy

All rights reserved.

No part of this publication may be reproduced, stored in a retrieval system, or transmitted, in any form or by any means, electronic, mechanical, photocopying, recording or otherwise, without the prior written permission of the presenters.

Melanie Kennedy asserts the moral right to be identified as the author of this work.

Presentation by *BookLeaf Publishing*

Web: www.bookleafpub.com

E-mail: info@bookleafpub.com

ISBN: 9789358736380

First edition 2023

For my father, who has stayed with me through the good and the bad.

ACKNOWLEDGEMENT

Thank you to everyone who got me to where I am today; you know who you are.

The Awkwardness of Conversation (and all the rules I have to remember)

Eye contact I have to maintain,
For a few seconds every few seconds,
But not too long, or else it's awkward…
Don't face away from a person,
Or let your eyes wander in a conversation,
Don't speak so loud – inside voice,
Even when you're excited.

Make sure not to interrupt,
But don't leave too long a pause,
Not everyone wants to hear,
About your interests.

You have to stay on topic otherwise,
People begin to doubt you are,
Paying attention even though you have heard
and,
Analysed every word.

It's exhausting to
Have a conversation

Advice You Didn't Ask For

You have to learn to like who you are
Or else you won't get very far
Do not tell others too much
Secrets, your life and such
You are the only person you can fully trust
Remember that – that's a must
Silence is golden and listening a skill
So is staying calm, keeping still
Hold the people you love tight
Because one day they will drift out of sight
Joined hands or paws will one day part
And take with them a piece of your heart
So, listen please, live well
What will happen next, only time will tell.

Gallery of the Heart

Welcome, welcome
Let's start over here –
Some tiny paws and yes!
Even little bird claws
What's that? Oh,
A hoof print, some tortoise steps.

Come back, that section is off limits!

Over here, we call this
The "Interest Section"
Some books over here,
Some writing over – hmm, where?
No, don't look there,
Here, here's some music,
Yes, the gallery has some wear and tear
No, no don't go…
We don't look here,
Come back into the light
That? That is fear.
Best left out of sight

Silent – yes, this part is silent.
Careful, those memories have gone astray,
The reaction is quite violent

Yes come away, come away,
Let this stay silent for another day.

Reality, Or Is It?

Reality, or is it?

Sometimes I feel like I'm watching a show
Or existing behind glass
Maybe I am, how can I know?
When will these feelings pass?

My hands are mine
I feel them on the keyboard
But no matter what I do all the time
These hands do not feel like mine.

I look at the face in the glass
The woman looks the same as me
But no matter what comes to pass
This face does not feel like mine.

The voice I hear is my voice.
There's no one else's it could be
But no matter what I tell myself
This voice does not feel like mine.

Overcoming

I found my story and read through
Maybe it will help you
You who may feel lost
Sad or lonely
Maybe you say to yourself
No one really knows me.

This was me
My thoughts, my words
When my entire world crumbled

I know I am a worthless shell of what I once was

I've lost so much weight
I feel numb all the time
We don't know how to fix ourselves

I'm broken with no hope or future
I'm just a burden
My brain feels screwed up
I want to go back to being me and I don't know how
Please don't leave me
I'm sorry

Be kind to yourself

Candle

I forced myself to acknowledge your death
And light the candle for you
I found it hard to take a breath
As it hit me – it was really true.

What was you is no longer
Now the grief is hitting me stronger

You have vanished
And your memories have been banished
To the furthest place away from me
So, I don't have to cope, so I don't have to see

That you are gone.

Building A Person

I have my masks on a coat hanger
I made one for every person I know
Daughter, friend, student, mentee
Who is the real me?

My personalities I keep in a jar
Am I funny?
Am I sarcastic?
Cynical? Moody?
I don't know how to just be.

Who is the real me?
I've gone so long with them all, you see,
I can't remember the real me.

Chic Café On A Rainy Day

Rainy day
Chic café
Wooden chair
Brick walls are bare
Black wooden tables
Branded labels
Modern? Cold?
Stylish? Bold?
Low-backed red couch
People with phones, all they do is slouch
Disconnect – pockets of talk
I need to get up and take a walk
Indie tunes
The clatter of spoons
House plants, a lamp
Umbrellas dripping, fabric damp
Pattern drawn in drinks
Cutlery thrown into sinks
Open windows – fresh air
In the corner, a loud pair
Old books
The barista looks
Up at the exposed pipes
Across the way a student types
I stand slowly and say goodbye
And watch as the rain begins to die.

Spiral Of Anxiety

Hello, there! Is my…
No, that's not right
Hello, my name is…
My brain is starting to spin
My heart has begun to soar
No! No! I won't let you win
I won't have anxiety anymore!

Did I do something wrong?
I have to stay strong
My body feels so cold
What is it I was told?
Calm, relax, breathe –
My thoughts begin to seethe
Spiralling, spiralling
Everything is too loud – STOP!
I feel like I'm about to drop
Why, oh why
Can't my thoughts ever stop?

Isolation In The Modern Age

How can I sit in
a room full of people and
feel so alone there?

A room is so loud
yet the talk is meaningless
just people on phones.

Look at me please look
Put the screen down and just talk
Why won't you just talk?

Trying To Go Home

being halfway across the world watching news reports
and the borders are closing and i'm in a country
where i don't belong and i'm scared
as i sit on a plane, filled with people in masks
want to get home, need to get home
on a full flight of students
trying to get back home
we've all been told to go home
and i still have one country to go
i have to go home.

waiting in an airport in Ireland
a ghost town, no one there
sat at a table watching half-empty planes
masks and no visible mouth in sight
talks of everything closing here too
i have to go home.

getting into my country
no checks, no comment
two weeks of quarantine
and then we're in lockdown
i'm trapped, i'm trapped at home.
months of panic and silence

racing thoughts and loneliness
shielding, shielding
spring turns to summer
summer turns to autumn
i'm still here.

university half open
autumn turns to winter
lockdown again
haven't seen the people i know for over a year
seen a few people
but not enough
please, i feel alone.

racing thoughts and little sleep
cold weather and dark days
they give us hope and take it back
i just want to feel like i'm home.

I Needed You

I have to say these words before they crush me
I have to stop this burning in my veins
I want to stop seeing your face
every time I close my eyes.
Why can't I say them?
Why?

You're beautiful
Sometimes the weight of life crushes me
and I feel like I'm drowning in all the emotions
around me
but you help me back up
you guide me through

all the words in the world failed me when
I needed them
every time I needed to step up
I couldn't do it
the words are failing me now

How can I say it?
Saying I love you is a lie
because I don't
not really
not enough

I will miss you?
I needed you?
I'm sorry.

You were there for me
When I needed you
But now I have to move on

Mind Mirror

Love is the greatest and cruellest gift humanity possesses
the ability to shatter someone to pieces or raise them up with a single word
Life is too busy, too many stresses
It isn't fair, haven't you heard?

Our minds reflect the worst parts of the soul
there are places in them that we can never face because of the pain
but our minds can reflect us as a whole
the best parts of us are there beneath the strain

Life is not fair
Love can cause pain
But I think it is better to care
Than exist inside a lonely brain

Message From A Ghost

In life,
I was a small, constant flame
the sort that would fade quietly into the eternal black
and nobody would even notice I was gone, save the few lives I touched.
We write our stories on the scars of the hearts we touch
Make sure that it's a good one

Cat Café

I went to a cat café today
Cats everywhere – sleeping, cleaning, wanting to play.
Fluffy cats trying to steal the cream from my drink
Cats who were secretly judging me, I think…

Cats meowing, cats purring
You could tell whenever a feed was occurring.
Cats darting in all directions to find a treat
I would have tripped over if I left my seat

Agents of chaos on four stumpy legs
It was funny to witness how one cat begs
Lying across the staircase to prevent an escape
Flattening itself out into a distinct pancake shape

I went to a cat café today
And what can I say?
The cats judged me and tried to steal my drink
But I'll be going again, I think.

Plastic Nation

I look down upon the tiny places,
Model cars, trains, people with no destination,
Tiny people with vague faces
A hollow, plastic nation.

Indistinct, no variation
Endless copies from the the same mould
I could not live in a plastic nation
In a world so incredibly cold.

I raise my head to look around
At the people above this miniature station
And realise without a sound
That I am the one living in a soulless, plastic nation.

Happiest Memories

I asked myself what would it be like to build machines,
That could show you your favourite dreams?
Or memories, but only the happiest ones...
Come on, let's see if this thing runs!

When I realised my mind was finally on the mend
My father happy
Making a huge decision, seeing it through to the end
When my pet bird walks and pretends to be snappy
Hugging the beings I care for the most
Walking across stage with my degree
When I get surprises from friends in the post
A friend taking me on a shopping spree.

Our memories remind us of times that are gone
But the only way to make more is to go on.

Memories of Summer

Long warm summer nights
Happy campfires and tall dark woods
Fireflies flickering

Escape From Freedom

The touch you are yearning for
the embrace you seek
is stopping you from seeing the future
approaching you.
But look at your wings
you can take flight
and escape to a place where
you can set us all free!

You must remember
do not lose your memories
through all the sorrow and the pain
go forward and break us free!

You sleep and want to stay
in my arms but only
you can go forward
a message will come to you
from your dreams.

Know this -
if I could stop time
I would keep you as fragile and warm
as you are at my side
but your fate is approaching

and must soon come to pass.

If there is real meaning
you must go on
the trial you face is the only way
we can be free.

Sorrow approaches
I will stand by you
but I am not the one you need
you must walk on alone

Go forward and break us free!

Voyager

At the end of the world
A voyager encased in metal
Set out from a world with a dead sea
To drift out into the heavens

In its heart, the final soul
Of a human lost to time

The lonely voyager floated
Proof that humanity existed
Long after the death of the world
Through the endless expanse of forever

Never to see the earth again

Keeper of memories
Bearer of pain
So many sacrifices made
To chase the dream of eternity

To All The Readers...

To all the readers
And those who understand this
Take care of yourself.

Milton Keynes UK
Ingram Content Group UK Ltd.
UKHW050003170224
437951UK00015B/747